Akiko and Amy Part 3

I Talk You Talk Press

CONTENTS

INTRODUCTION

This is Part 3 of Akiko and Amy's Story. The story starts in the graded reader *Akiko and Amy Part 1*.

1. AKIKO GOES FOR A JOB INTERVIEW

Akiko wanted a job. She felt bad. Her friend Amy was a writer. Amy wrote a book and a company wanted to publish it. Akiko didn't do anything.

What kind of job could I do? thought Akiko. *I am a good cook. I studied cooking. But it is difficult to get a chef's job. I want to be home at night. I want to be home on Saturdays and Sundays. If I am a chef I will have to work at night and on the weekends. Then I will not be home when Seiji is home. I love my husband. I want to spend time with him. My dream is to have my own restaurant but that is impossible.*

Seiji, Akiko's husband, works in an office downtown. One Wednesday, he didn't get home until 10:00pm. He was tired. Akiko prepared his bath. She served dinner. Seiji thought that Akiko was very quiet.

"Did you have a good day?" he asked.

"Yes. It was OK. I did some cleaning and I helped a neighbour clean the grounds around the apartments. Amy is very busy now so I didn't talk with her today," answered Akiko.

"What's wrong Akiko?" Seiji asked.

Akiko sat on the floor opposite Seiji. "I was thinking. I would like to have a job. What do you think?"

Seiji thought, *My life is very comfortable. I have a beautiful wife. She does everything very well. She is always at home when I come home. We have enough money. Someday we will buy a house and we will have children. I don't want anything to change.*

Then he looked at Akiko. She was very quiet and unhappy.

"Maybe a job is a good idea," he said. "What kind of job would you like?"

"I would like to own a restaurant," said Akiko. "But that is an impossible dream."

Seiji smiled. "I can't make your dream come true. I don't have enough money for you to buy a restaurant, but maybe I can do something to help you."

Akiko was surprised. "What can you do?"

"You make a beautiful lunch box for me every day. But other men in my office are not so lucky. They go out to eat lunch in a restaurant. There is a small restaurant near my office. Many people from my office go there for lunch. Today Wada san said that the restaurant would be closed for a month. The man who owns the restaurant is sick. His doctor says he must rest. He has no one to cook for him so he must close the restaurant until he is well again. Tomorrow I will go and talk to the man in the restaurant. Maybe you could work there for a few weeks."

Akiko smiled. "Seiji you are a wonderful husband," she said.

The next day Seiji went to see the man in the restaurant. His name was Kimura.

Seiji said to Mr Kimura, "My wife is a very good cook. She went to cooking school. She would like to work. If you can pay her a little money, she will come and cook in your restaurant at lunchtime. You can take a rest."

Mr Kimura looked very tired. "Maybe that's a good idea," he said. "Please ask your wife to come to see me."

Akiko went to see Mr Kimura at 10.30am. Mr Kimura and Akiko sat in the kitchen. Mr Kimura asked her many questions. "Can you cook everything on my menu?" he asked.

Akiko looked at the menu. The menu was very short. If you went to Mr Kimura's restaurant you could have curry and rice, or noodles. There were two different kinds of curry. There were four different kinds of noodles.

"I can cook these," she said.

"Can you take orders, cook, take money and clean?" asked Mr Kimura. "This is a small, cheap restaurant. I do everything alone."

"If I watch you working, I will know how to do all the jobs in this restaurant by myself," answered Akiko.

"Hmm. I don't know," said Mr Kimura. "You are young and

pretty. I don't think you know how to work hard."

Akiko was upset. "Please! Let me watch you today. Then I can come tomorrow and help you. You don't have to pay me."

Mr Kimura was very ill. He felt very tired. He wanted to take a rest but he didn't believe Akiko would work hard.

"I don't think so," he said. "I'm sorry, but you are not a good type of person for this restaurant. It is eleven o' clock. I must start cooking for the people who will come for lunch. Please leave now."

Akiko bowed. "I understand. Thank you for talking to me."

Akiko walked out of the kitchen into the restaurant. She was crying. She opened the door of the restaurant. Suddenly she heard a shout and a loud noise from the kitchen. Akiko went back into the kitchen. Mr Kimura was lying on the floor. His eyes were closed. Akiko took out her mobile phone and called the ambulance. The ambulance came quickly. Mr Kimura's eyes were still closed. The ambulance men asked Akiko, "What happened?"

"I don't know," said Akiko. "I know he was ill. I know his doctor told him to rest. I came to talk to him. I was walking out of the restaurant when I heard a loud noise. I came back. He was lying on the floor. That's all I know."

"You should call his family," said one of the ambulance men. "He is very ill. We will take him to the hospital."

The ambulance men took Mr Kimura away. Akiko did not know what to do. She called Seiji. She told him that she talked to Mr Kimura. She told him that Mr Kimura became very ill. She told him she called the ambulance. She did not tell Seiji that Mr Kimura did not want her to work in his restaurant. Seiji was very happy about his clever plan. Akiko did not want him to know his plan had not worked.

"The ambulance men told me to call his family. But I don't know anything about him. What should I do?"

"I will ask Wada san if he knows about Kimura san's family. He has been going to that restaurant for a long time. I will call the hospital. You had a bad morning. Go home and relax. I will do everything."

Akiko was still in the restaurant kitchen. She looked around. Mr Kimura had prepared everything for lunch. There were bags of curry on the table. There was a big dish of cut cabbage. The light on the rice cooker was green. The rice was cooked.

Akiko looked at her mobile phone. It was 11:40am.

I will not go home, thought Akiko. *I will stay and cook lunch for the customers. Mr Kimura will know that I can work hard. He will let me work here and he can take a rest.*

Akiko was excited. It was her dream to have a restaurant. For just one lunchtime, her dream would come true.

Akiko worked very hard. At 12:05pm people started to come into the restaurant for lunch. They were office workers. They wanted to eat lunch quickly. They did not want to wait. Akiko ran from the kitchen to the restaurant to the cash desk. She got very tired. Some people were angry when Akiko was slow. One of the angry people was Mr Wada. Mr Wada works in the same office as Seiji.

"I'm sorry," said Akiko. "Kimura san got sick this morning. I'm trying to help him. Please be patient."

At 1:30pm the last people left the restaurant. Akiko sat down in the kitchen. She was very tired. There were many dishes to wash and then she had to clean the restaurant and the kitchen. But Akiko was very happy.

I can do this, she thought. *Tomorrow I will be much quicker. I will help Kimura san while he has a rest.*

Akiko thought the cooking was very easy. Mr Kimura used packets of soup for the noodles. He used curry sauce in bags. Almost everything on the menu was made in a factory. Mr Kimura cut cabbage and cooked noodles and rice. He heated the soup and the curry sauce.

I could make more interesting food, she thought.

Akiko finished cleaning. She put the dishes away. She took the money from the cash box and counted it. Her telephone rang. It was Seiji.

"Wada san knows Kimura san's son. He lives in Osaka. Wada san has called him. You don't have to worry. I hope you feel OK now you are at home."

"But I'm not at home Seiji. I stayed at the restaurant. I cooked lunch for many people. Then I cleaned everything. But I have a problem. I don't know what to do with the money and I don't know where the keys are. I can't lock the restaurant."

"You stayed? You used the kitchen? You used Kimura san's food? You took money? Oh, Akiko. Maybe that was a bad idea!" Seiji was shouting.

Akiko was frightened. Seiji never shouted at her. "But Seiji......" she cried.

Seiji was quiet. Then he said, "Maybe it's OK. I'm sorry I shouted. You were going to work for Kimura san anyway. You started a little early, that's all."

"But Seiji!" Akiko was very worried now. "He didn't want me! I didn't get the job!"

2. MR KIMURA'S LUNCHTIME RESTAURANT

Akiko was waiting at Mr Kimura's lunchtime restaurant. Seiji said that he would come after work and meet her there. They had to make a plan.

That morning, Akiko met Mr Kimura. Mr Kimura wanted someone to work in his restaurant because he needed to take a rest. Akiko wanted the job. But Mr Kimura didn't like Akiko. He said he didn't want her to work in his restaurant.

When Akiko was leaving, Mr Kimura fell on the floor. He was very sick. Akiko called the ambulance. The ambulance men took Mr Kimura to the hospital. It was almost lunchtime. Akiko had an idea. She would look after the restaurant. She would cook the food in the kitchen. She would sell lunch to customers. She would clean. Then Mr Kimura would know she was a good worker. He would give her the job.

Akiko did everything. She was very happy. But she didn't know what to do with the money. She didn't have the keys to lock the restaurant. She talked to her husband, Seiji. Seiji was angry. He thought Akiko's idea was very bad. It was wrong for her to use Mr Kimura's restaurant. It was wrong to use his kitchen, take his food and sell lunch to his customers.

Now Akiko was very worried and she was very unhappy. She loved Seiji very much and he was angry with her. *I am so stupid,* she thought.

Seiji arrived at the restaurant at 6:30pm.

"Oh, Seiji! I am so sorry!" said Akiko. "I was stupid and I have made a lot of trouble!"

"Maybe it is not so bad," said Seiji. "I asked Wada san for the telephone number of Kimura san's son in Osaka. I called him. He is coming here now to see his father in the hospital. He said there are keys for the restaurant in an old box. It is in the cupboard under the rice cooker.

He said, "Please thank your wife. Tell her to take the money home."

Akiko was very happy! "That's wonderful! He was not angry about what I did?"

"He doesn't know," said Seiji. "I didn't tell him. I told him you came for a job interview. He thinks his father gave you a job."

"Oh, no!" said Akiko. "His father will tell him he didn't like me! He will say he did not give me a job! Then he will be angry with you and me. He will tell Wada san. There will be terrible trouble!"

"I know," said Seiji. "But that trouble will not come until tomorrow."

Akiko and Seiji took the money. They locked the restaurant and walked to the car park. Seiji put the keys for the restaurant in his pocket.

"I forgot to tell you," he said. "Kimura san's son asked if you could work in the restaurant tomorrow. He said to use some of the money to buy food for lunch tomorrow. He said he would pay you wages. He said you must keep receipts for everything."

That night, Akiko could not sleep. She was so worried. She had tried to get a job and she had done everything wrong. Mr Kimura would tell his son that she didn't get the job. Then the son would tell Mr Wada, and Seiji would have trouble at work. She must go to the hospital very early. She must tell Mr Kimura's son what she had done. She must say she was very sorry. That was the right thing to do.

The next morning Akiko got up early. She made breakfast for Seiji and she made his lunch box. She was worried. Seiji was worried too. But he tried to make Akiko feel happier. "Don't worry. Maybe everything will be OK."

Akiko wanted to believe Seiji but she didn't think everything would be OK. She put the money and the keys in an envelope. She would go to the hospital and give them to Mr Kimura's son.

Then the telephone rang. Seiji went to answer it. Akiko tried to listen. Seiji came back to the table and sat down. "That was Kimura san's son," he said.

"Oh, no!" cried Akiko. "Is he very angry?"

"No. Maybe he is sad. His father died late last night. He says the restaurant cannot open today. He asked if you could please put a sign on the door to say his father died."

"Oh!" said Akiko. "Does he know what I did?"

"No. I don't think so," said Seiji. "Maybe his father didn't speak before he died. I will make the notice and put it on the door of the shop. The restaurant is very close to my office. It will be easy for me."

Akiko felt very bad. Mr Kimura had not been nice to her. But he was an old man and he was sick. Now he had died.

The funeral was the next day. Seiji didn't go but Akiko thought that she should go.

After the funeral, everyone was standing outside the funeral hall. Mr Wada came to talk to her. "Are you Yamamoto Seiji's wife?" he asked.

"Yes, I am," answered Akiko.

"I am Wada. I work with your husband. Kimura san would like to talk to you."

Akiko followed Mr Wada.

"Do you know Kimura san's son well?" she asked Mr Wada.

"We were at school together."

Mr Wada introduced Akiko to Mr Kimura. "Thank you for helping my father," said Mr Kimura. "No one knew he was so sick. It was a big shock when he died."

"I only met him once," said Akiko quietly. Mr Kimura's son didn't know that his father didn't want her to work in the restaurant!

"But you tried to help him. I think you did a good thing for him. I want to come and talk to you. Will your husband be home tomorrow?"

"Yes. It is Saturday. He often works on Saturdays. But tomorrow I think he will be at home," said Akiko.

"Can I come to your apartment tomorrow?"

"Uh, yes," Akiko answered. "I am very sorry your father died."

Mr Kimura's son bowed and went away.

When Seiji came home that night, Akiko talked to him..

"This is a terrible mess," she said. "What should I do?"

"Don't do anything," said Seiji. "It will not help anyone if you tell the truth now."

Akiko agreed that she would not say anything but she felt very bad.

The next day was Saturday. Mr Kimura came to Akiko's apartment.

Akiko made tea. Mr Kimura talked to Seiji.

"Now my father is dead. I must go back to Osaka, but first I must arrange everything. My father did not own the restaurant. The building belongs to Wada san's family. My father owned the things inside the restaurant but he rented the space from the Wada family. My friend Wada says that he will rent the space to your wife. If you pay me for the things in the restaurant, you can have the restaurant."

"You are very kind," said Seiji.

"No. I don't think so," answered Mr Kimura. "My father's restaurant was not successful. He didn't make a lot of money. I don't think he would have paid your wife a good salary. My plan is very convenient and easy for me. But you will have to be very clever to make money from the restaurant."

"How much rent does Wada san want?" asked Seiji.

"The building is old. The Wada family does not want to spend any money renovating it. They don't think anyone else will want to rent it. He will ask for the same rent my father paid."

"How much money do you want for the things inside the shop?" Seiji asked.

"Oh, I don't know. But maybe 200,000 yen?" Mr Kimura looked rich. He had very expensive clothes and a gold watch. Akiko thought maybe he didn't care about the restaurant. He just wanted an easy way, so he didn't have to do anything.

Akiko wanted to speak. She coughed. "Uh. Excuse me."

"Yes?" Mr Kimura looked at her.

"I would like to change the style of the restaurant and the menu," said Akiko quietly. "Would that be OK?"

Mr Kimura laughed. "Do anything! Maybe you can make more money than my father!"

"We must talk about this," said Seiji. "And I must speak to Wada san. Can you wait for a week?"

"No," said Mr Kimura. "I will go back to Osaka tomorrow. You must decide before then."

"OK," said Seiji. "Can you give me your telephone number? I will call you tonight or tomorrow morning."

3. PAPERWORK

Seiji and Akiko talked about Mr Kimura's plan. Seiji did not want Akiko to have a restaurant. He liked his life and his beautiful wife. He did not want to be married to a businesswoman. But he could see that Akiko wanted this chance very much. He thought if he did not help Akiko, perhaps she would stop loving him.

"Why don't you try?" he said to Akiko.

"Really?" Akiko was very happy. "But Seiji, I will need to spend some money. We have to pay Kimura san and we will have to pay Wada san too."

"Well, what about the money for our honeymoon? Maybe our honeymoon can be delayed. Then you could use that money."

When Akiko and Seiji got married, Seiji had just started a new job. He couldn't ask for vacation time. Akiko and Seiji decided to wait and save money. Then when Seiji could take a vacation and they had enough money, they would have a honeymoon in Europe.

Akiko knew that Seiji wanted to go to Europe very much. He often talked about it.

"Are you sure Seiji? We have been talking about our honeymoon trip to Europe for a long time. I don't want you to give it up."

Seiji smiled at Akiko. "I am not giving up on our honeymoon plan. We will go later. That's all. I don't think you will need all the money we have saved. So maybe you should take half for your restaurant."

"That would be wonderful!" said Akiko.

"OK. I'll call Wada san now."

"I'm going to go and tell Amy!" Akiko ran out the door to visit

Amy.

Seiji called Mr Wada.

Mr Wada agreed to rent the restaurant space.

"I know it is your wife's business, but I will only rent the space to you. You must sign the papers for the lease," he told Seiji. "How long do you want the lease to be?"

Seiji didn't know if Akiko was really serious about the restaurant. He thought maybe the idea was like a hobby because Akiko was bored. He thought she might quit after a few months. But Seiji knew that Akiko would have to pay the rent until the end of the lease.

"Could we agree to six months?" he asked Mr Wada. "If my wife can make a success in that time, then we could make a new agreement."

"If your wife is successful, then the new rent will be higher," said Mr Wada.

"Hmmm." Seiji thought about this. "But still, business is risky and my wife has no experience, so I think six months is OK."

Mr Wada and Seiji agreed to meet at the restaurant the next day.

Then Akiko came back. "Amy thinks it is wonderful! She is so busy now, but later she will help me!"

Seiji told Akiko that Mr Wada would rent the restaurant space, but he would only sign an agreement with Seiji. Akiko was angry.

"It's my restaurant! Why is he so horrible?"

"Because you are so young and pretty," Seiji told his wife. "Never mind, the first agreement is only for six months. When Wada san sees that the restaurant is successful, he will do business with you. I promise you. You can sign the lease next time!"

The next two weeks were very busy for Akiko. There was a lot of paperwork. Mr Kimura's son had closed the restaurant. He had cancelled the license. Akiko had to do all the paperwork to get a new one. She went from the city office to the prefectural office and to the bank many times. She had to learn all the public health rules. She had to show her cooking certificate to the prefectural office. She had to check out the public health and fire safety requirements. There would be an inspection of the restaurant. If the restaurant did not pass the inspection she would not get a license.

She was lucky, because in her city there was a business association that helped people to start new businesses. They were very kind. But there was still a lot to do.

Akiko got very tired. She missed Amy. Amy was very busy too. Sometimes they talked on the telephone but they didn't meet. Finally, Akiko had finished almost everything. But she was worried. She had spent more than half the money in the honeymoon account. She didn't say anything to Seiji. But she was worried. She needed to hire someone to work in the restaurant and she needed money to pay them. She also needed to buy food.

She talked to the staff at the new business association. The man said to her, "Many new small companies fail in the first year. People never understand how much money they need to start a business. They have problems with cash flow because in the beginning, you have to spend money and no money is coming back in."

One night, Dick and Seiji decided to take their wives out for dinner.

"Akiko and Amy have both been working hard," said Dick. "We should go out and relax on Saturday night. Also Amy and I want to talk to you about something."

I wonder what they want to talk about, thought Seiji. *I hope they are not planning to return to America. Akiko and I will miss them.*

They went to an Indian restaurant. Amy was very cheerful. "I've almost finished everything," she said. "Now I can have some free time."

The food was delicious, but Akiko didn't eat. She was very quiet.

"How is the restaurant business?" asked Dick.

"It's difficult," said Akiko. "I was very shocked when I saw the rules for public health and fire safety. Mr Kimura should not have had a license. The restaurant didn't obey the rules. I had to get fire extinguishers and a new floor for the kitchen. I have to buy a new refrigerator. The insurance is very expensive too. Then I had to pay for a license. The inspectors will come next week. The restaurant doesn't look very nice, but I think it will pass."

"It sounds expensive," said Amy. "Do you have enough money?"

"If Akiko needs more money, we have it," said Seiji.

"Oh, Seiji," said Akiko. "I don't want to take more money out of the honeymoon account. But I might have to. I'm really sorry."

"Maybe you don't have to," said Dick. "Amy and I have an idea."

"You see," explained Amy. "We saved some money to take a vacation in America. But now it seems we won't need it. Dick will take some students to America for language study. The university will pay for Dick's airfare. Another teacher is going too. So Dick doesn't have to come back with the students. Then, there is my mother's wedding! She and Homer will pay for me to go to their wedding. They will pay for Dick too. But Dick doesn't need an air ticket. So Homer sent us some spending money. He said we should travel around America and enjoy ourselves. He has an apartment in New York and he said we could stay there. Our vacation in America will be almost free and so we have some extra money."

Amy stopped. She looked at Dick.

"So we have something to ask you," said Dick. "Amy wants to take a break from writing. She would like to try something different."

"I want to ask you Akiko, if I can be your junior partner." Amy looked worried. "It will always be your restaurant, but I would love to be part of it. What do you think?"

Akiko was very surprised. "Really?"

"Yes, really. But if you don't want me to join you, I will understand."

"Of course I want you to join me. We will have so much fun!"

Everyone was happy. Dick ordered champagne. The waiter poured the champagne and they lifted their glasses for a toast.

"To the future success of ...," Dick stopped. "Akiko. What is the name of the restaurant?"

Akiko laughed. "I don't know. I have been so busy I haven't thought about a name yet."

"Well then." Dick lifted his champagne glass again. "To the success of the 'no name' restaurant!"

4. BEFORE AND AFTER

Akiko decided to call the restaurant *Tuscany*.

"Seiji and I want to visit Tuscany on our honeymoon trip to Europe," said Akiko. "I used some of the money we saved for the trip for this restaurant. So I think it's a good idea."

Amy liked the name too. "I have never been to Tuscany, but I believe it is very beautiful. People are interested in Italy and most people like Italian food."

They were working hard. They decided to open their restaurant on April first. There were many things to do.

They cleaned the restaurant. Mr Kimura had been old, and tired and sick. He had not cleaned the kitchen or the restaurant very well. When it was clean, Amy and Akiko looked around.

"It doesn't look very nice," said Akiko.

"No," Amy agreed. "Maybe we should paint the walls?"

"Paint the walls?" Akiko was surprised. "But it will cost a lot of money."

"I don't think it will cost so much. We can buy paint in the hardware store."

"But we have to pay a painting company to do it." Akiko was worried about money.

"No way!" answered Amy. "Dick can do it."

"Can Dick paint walls?"

"Of course. I will ask him."

Amy asked Dick. He said he would be happy to help.

Seiji asked Mr Wada if they could paint the walls and ceiling of the

15

restaurant.

Mr Wada said, "Yes. You can do that. But I will not pay for anything. If you want to renovate, you must pay."

Amy and Akiko had fun choosing a colour scheme.

They chose pale yellow for the walls. Dick said he would paint the ceiling too. He said the rooms would look brighter if the ceiling was white. Dick spent two weekends painting. Seiji helped him on Sundays.

Akiko called her mother. She asked her mother to send her old sewing machine. Amy went to a discount shop and bought blue and white check fabric. Amy made tablecloths for all the tables. They found cheap paper napkins on the Internet. Amy and Akiko ordered a big box of blue paper napkins.

Dick has a friend who owns a travel agency. He emailed his friend and asked for some posters of scenery in Europe.

Dick's friend sent a roll of posters. The posters showed beautiful gardens and beaches in France and Italy. Then Dick found some cheap frames at an art shop. He framed the posters to make pictures for the walls. When all the painting was finished, they hung the poster pictures on the walls and put the new tablecloths on the tables.

On Sunday night they sat and drank a bottle of wine together in the empty restaurant. It looked wonderful.

"Now this is a dramatic before and after!" said Seiji.

Akiko laughed.

"What's the joke?" asked Dick.

"There is a programme on Japanese television. In English, the title means: dramatic before and after. It's a programme about home renovation. I love watching it," explained Akiko.

The restaurant looked bright and cheerful. The kitchen was clean but Akiko and Amy still had many things to do.

Akiko was making a menu for the restaurant.

"We want to keep the old customers," she told Amy. "So I will cook the same things as Mr Kimura did. So that is curry rice and noodles."

"It's a bit boring," said Amy.

"Oh yes. I know. But some people don't like new food. Some people like to have noodles or curry and rice for lunch every day. We can have some new and interesting meals on the menu, for new customers."

Akiko and Amy decided to add some soups, salads and sandwiches to the menu.

"Some younger people might like those," said Akiko. "We want our restaurant to be a success. We want all the old customers, but we want new customers too."

Akiko knows a lot about cooking food. But when she was at cooking school she did not study baking cakes, or cookies or bread.

Luckily Amy is very good at baking. Amy and Akiko decided that they would start working every morning at 8:00am. Akiko would prepare everything for the noodles, curry and rice, soup, salads and sandwiches. Amy would make bread, cakes, muffins and cookies. The restaurant would open at 11:30am and close at 2:00pm.

From 2:00pm to 4:00pm, they would clean and prepare some food for the next day. The restaurant would be open from Monday to Friday.

"This is the office area of the city," said Akiko. "There are not so many people here on Saturdays and Sundays."

"And we will need a rest," laughed Amy.

Amy and Akiko went to the restaurant every day. On Saturdays, Dick came to help them. Sometimes Seiji did not have to go to work. He helped at the restaurant too.

Amy used her computer and blue paper to make menu cards. She made a beautiful poster for the window with the menu and prices on it.

Akiko practiced all the dishes she planned to make. She found good shops to buy the ingredients.

"I don't want to pay too much for the ingredients," she said. "But the quality must be good."

Akiko and Amy bought a freezer. They decided to cook some dishes, like curry, ahead of time and freeze them. Akiko cooked a lot and they filled the freezer.

"When we are very busy, it will be useful," she said.

By the middle of March, everything was almost finished.

They were all very happy and excited.

"Only two more weeks and we will be business women!" said Amy.

"Your restaurant will be a great success!" said Dick "We will have lots of money. Then maybe I can stop working."

5. THE FIRST WEEK IN APRIL

Akiko could not sleep the night before. She was very excited. The next day, her dream would come true. She would have a restaurant.

Akiko and Amy went to *Tuscany* very early. Amy had bought flowers. She put them in vases on each table. Akiko cleaned the windows again. Everything was bright and clean and pretty. The glass case near the kitchen was filled with salads and sandwiches. The kitchen smelt delicious.

Akiko's mother could not come for the opening day but she sent beautiful flowers and a good luck message. Linda and Homer sent flowers too. Jacob, Dick's father, and his new wife Maria sent a good luck email.

Seiji was at work but Dick said he would come as soon as his classes at the university were finished. Everything was ready

At 11:30am, Amy sat at the cash desk and watched the door. It was cold and raining. There were not many people on the street. The restaurant was in the middle of the business district. There were banks, bars, restaurants and convenience stores, but it was not a shopping area. Akiko waited in the kitchen for their first order.

At 11:45 she came out to talk to Amy. "Has anyone looked at the menu in the window?" she asked.

"No. No one has stopped. There are almost no people out there. Just some business people walking past very quickly," answered Amy.

Akiko sat down next to Amy. "There will be a lot of people soon. It's almost lunchtime," she said.

Akiko and Amy sat quietly and waited. After 12:00, there were many more people on the street. Some walked towards the restaurant. They looked at the menu. They looked inside the restaurant, but then they walked away.

When Dick arrived at 1:00pm he found Akiko and Amy sitting together in an empty restaurant. "What's wrong?" he asked. "What happened?"

"We don't know," answered Amy. "Some people looked in. Some people read the menu, but no one came inside."

"What kind of people were they?" Dick couldn't understand.

"They were men in suits. Businessmen. Akiko thinks two or three of them might have been customers of Mr Kimura's. She remembers their faces from the day she cooked for Mr Kimura. The day he became very ill," said Amy.

"One of them was Wada san," said Akiko. "He was with two other men. They looked in but then they went away."

"How about young people?" asked Dick. He was very worried. Amy and Akiko looked so disappointed.

"We haven't seen any young people" answered Amy.

"Well it's cold and wet today," said Dick. "Perhaps people are staying in their offices. Tomorrow will be better. You wait and see!"

At 2:00pm, Akiko and Amy sadly threw the salads into the garbage. Akiko put the curry and soups in the refrigerator.

She smiled at Amy. "Dick is right. Tomorrow will be better."

The next day, the weather was beautiful. But still no one came into the restaurant. The day after that was the same. The flowers in the vases died. Amy threw them away.

In the evenings, Akiko and Amy sat in their apartments and stared at the television. Dick called Seiji and said, "I will meet you for a drink after work tonight. Please call me when you are free."

Seiji called Dick about 8:00pm and they met in a small bar near Seiji's office.

"What's the problem?" asked Dick.

"I don't know," said Seiji drinking his whisky very quickly. "Maybe someone has said something bad about the restaurant."

"But why?" Dick ordered another beer. "Why would anyone say something bad?"

"Maybe Wada san has said something. He doesn't like me."

"But Seiji," Dick answered. "If the restaurant is a success, Wada san will get more money. The rent will increase if the restaurant is a success."

"I don't know," said Seiji. He was tired and worried.

"What about the younger people who work in offices? Why don't they go to the restaurant? I thought they would be interested in something new."

"Maybe it looks too expensive."

Seiji and Dick got very drunk. They had to take a taxi home. But by the time they left the bar, they had made a plan.

The next day and the day after that, Dick rode his bicycle around the streets near the restaurant during lunchtime. He watched the people coming out of offices at lunchtime. He watched where they went to buy lunch. He and Seiji thought that Mr Kimura's customers probably worked nearby. He followed groups of office workers. Many men in suits walked to a restaurant in the next street. It looked just like Mr Kimura's old restaurant, but it was further away.

They would rather walk further than go to Tuscany, thought Dick. *I wonder why.*

Most of the younger office workers went to convenience stores and bought bread or sandwiches and drinks. They sat in the park or took them back to their offices.

Seiji called a friend from his schooldays. His friend worked at a newspaper. He asked him about advertising. It was very expensive. Seiji ordered a small advertisement for a week. He was very happy to help Akiko.

The next day he bought a newspaper. He looked very hard at the newspaper. It took him a long time to find the advertisement. It was very small. He thought, *No one will see this. We need a very big advertisement but that will cost too much money.*

He showed the advertisement to Akiko.

"I'm sure that advertising is a good idea," he said. "We should take the rest of the honeymoon money and pay for a nice big advertisement with pictures."

Akiko did not agree. "We have spent too much money already. I have to buy new food every day and we have no customers. I don't know what is wrong."

"You must not give up," said Seiji. "A new business is very difficult. You must be patient."

Dick said the same thing to Amy. Dick thought that the restaurant was in the wrong place. There were no customers for this kind of restaurant. But he didn't say that to Amy. He thought Akiko and Amy had worked so hard. He didn't like to see them so sad.

Every day Akiko and Amy cooked and cleaned and waited for customers. Every day was the same. At 2:00pm they threw the food away.

6. THE SECOND WEEK IN APRIL

The weekend was terrible. The restaurant was not open but Akiko and Amy thought about it all the time.

"This week will be better," said Amy. They tried very hard. Amy bought new flowers. They made bread, sandwiches, salads and cakes. Akiko didn't make any more curry or soup. She took containers from the freezer. She was trying to save money.

On Tuesday, two tourists came into the restaurant. Akiko heard the door open and ran to the kitchen door. *Now, maybe our luck will change! Our first customers!* she thought.

Amy smiled at them. "Welcome! Where would you like to sit?"

"Oh, we've eaten lunch," said one of the tourists. She took a map out of her bag. "But we would like directions to the museum. I think we're lost."

Akiko came out of the kitchen and showed the tourists the way to the museum.

She sat at a table and Amy sat down too. "What are we going to do?" she asked Amy.

"Well. Why don't we close early today? Let's eat some lunch and go to the museum. We need a change."

Akiko agreed. She took salads and sandwiches from the glass case. Amy made coffee and they ate their lunch.

"Maybe we will have to give up," said Akiko. "We should talk to Dick and Seiji tonight. I know we have spent a lot of money and that would be wasted. But every day we are open, we spend more money."

They started taking the salads and sandwiches out to the garbage bags in the kitchen. In the kitchen Akiko laughed. "I hope you and Dick like curry. We have a freezer full of curry. We will have to eat it all."

Just then, they both heard the door open.

Amy went out to look. *More tourists wanting directions,* she thought.

But it was a group of older women. There were six of them.

"I know this is a lunch restaurant, but could we just have coffee?" asked one of the women.

"Of course," said Amy. "Please come to this big table over here."

Amy went into the kitchen to tell Akiko. Akiko made coffee. Amy went to the display case and took out her latest cake. She took it to the kitchen.

"We can't sell this but we can give it away. I think we should give them some cake" said Amy.

Amy cut some of the cake into small pieces. She arranged the pieces on a plate with blue napkins. Akiko took out the coffee and Amy followed with the cake.

"We didn't order cake!" said one of the women.

"I know," smiled Amy. "But I made it. I think it is good. Please try some. It is a small gift from us to you."

The women seemed happy to have some free cake. When they left, they thanked Amy. They paid for the coffee.

"Thank you for coming. I hope we will see you again," said Amy.

"We usually go to a coffee shop near the lake," said one of the women. "We only came here today because their car park was full."

"Could you find a parking space here?" Amy was surprised.

"I have a parking space next door," one of the other women said.

It was another terrible week at the restaurant. After the excitement of the ladies coming for coffee on Tuesday, no one else came in.

7. LUNCH WITH MR WADA

The next Monday, Mr Wada came up to Seiji's desk.

"Would you have lunch with me today, Yamamoto san?"

Seiji was surprised. Mr Wada was senior to Seiji. Usually he was not nice to Seiji.

Then Seiji thought, *Someone has talked to him. He knows the restaurant is not a success. Wada san is going to tell me that Akiko must close her restaurant. This is terrible!*

"Yes of course Wada san. It is very good of you to ask me to join you. Thank you."

"OK," said Mr Wada. "I'll meet you outside the building at twelve fifteen."

"Certainly Wada san, Thank you. I'll be there."

Seiji decided not to call Akiko and tell her. He did not want to make Akiko unhappy.

Akiko and Amy were at the restaurant. They were thinking about closing the restaurant. If they closed the restaurant, they could sell some things, such as the freezer. They hoped to get some of the money back.

Seiji had a lunch box. Akiko made a beautiful lunch box for him every day. Seiji went to see his friend Hiroshi Ohara in the accounting office. Hiroshi is single. He doesn't have a lot of money. He can't go to a restaurant every day. Usually Hiroshi and Seiji eat lunch together. Seiji has a nice lunch box but Hiroshi makes instant noodles. Seiji said to Hiroshi, "Do you have any chopsticks in your desk drawer?"

"Oh yes," said Hiroshi. Seiji gave him his lunchbox.

"My wife made this for me today but now I am going out for lunch. So I don't need it. Please enjoy it. My wife is a good cook."

Hiroshi was very pleased. "Thank you!" he said. "Why are you going out for lunch?"

"Wada san has invited me."

"What!" Hiroshi was surprised.

At lunchtime, Seiji was very nervous.

When he met Mr Wada, the older man said, "We will go to *Murakami*. I made a reservation."

Seiji was shocked. *Murakami* was the most expensive restaurant in the city. Seiji was worried.

Do I have enough money to pay? he wondered.

They walked to *Murakami*. The restaurant was very beautiful. They had a private room. Outside the windows was a very small but very beautiful garden. Normally Seiji would have enjoyed it very much.

Mr Wada ordered sake. The food was wonderful. After they had been eating for a few minutes, Mr Wada started speaking.

"Mr Kimura came to see me last week. Do you remember him? He is the son of the man who had the restaurant."

"Yes Wada san. I remember him well."

"He wants to come back from Osaka. He wants to have the restaurant back. He asked me to tell you to leave."

"But Wada san. We have a six month lease."

"I know. But the restaurant is not doing well. Kimura san knows this. He will give you back the 200,000 yen you paid him for the equipment in the restaurant. He has asked me to break our agreement. He is sure you will agree."

"Wada san. What did you say?"

"I told him 'no'."

"Why?" Seiji was amazed.

"I knew Kimura san at school. But he was not my friend. He never visited his father. When his father died he came back. But he was not interested in the restaurant. He was only interested in his father's money.

"I wondered why he wanted to come back now. So I asked questions. Kimura san lost his job in Osaka. That's why he wants the restaurant back. But he lost his job because he did something bad. The company did not want to tell the police, but they told him to go.

"Maybe I would have broken the agreement with you. I know your wife must have money troubles. But my mother has another opinion. She has been to your wife's restaurant. She went with her friends. They only drank coffee. She said she felt sorry for your wife and her American friend. There were no customers and they worked so hard. She said the room was very pretty. Also, I am a businessman. Your wife will always pay the rent. I do not want to rent space in my family's building to a man like Kimura san. He might not pay me."

The waitress came in with some more food. When she left the room, Mr Wada said,

"I live in my family home with my mother, my wife and three daughters. You can understand why I go out to study English. It is very difficult to keep five women happy. I can understand why you helped your wife to start her restaurant. I can understand it must be difficult now for you."

"Wada san, you are being very kind. But why?"

Mr Wada smiled. "To tell the truth, it is not me. It is my mother. My mother told me to do this.

"My parents started a small clothes store. Twenty years later, they had three clothing stores and a factory that made school uniforms. Everyone admired my father. They said he was a very clever businessman. It was not true. It was my mother. She is a very clever woman. In those days women with children were not expected to manage companies. So everyone thought it must be my father."

"But Wada san. What happened to the stores and the factory?"

"Ten years ago, my mother wanted to retire. I had an office job and was not interested in the clothes stores. So she sold them and bought buildings with the money.

"She is still very active. She often goes out. She and her friends often go to restaurants or to the movies. Of course she knows about the restaurant. She wants to help your wife and the American woman. She says they have made some mistakes. If they want her help, she will meet them at the restaurant tomorrow at eleven o' clock."

8. MR WADA'S MOTHER

Mrs Wada came to the restaurant at 11:00am. She was old. Akiko thought she must be eighty years old or more. She was very elegant. Her clothes were beautiful. Akiko made coffee.

"Please sit down," said Mrs Wada. "I came to this restaurant with my friends last week."

"I remember," said Amy.

"I will give you some advice. I was in business myself for many years. Not a restaurant. Clothes. We had three clothes stores; a family clothes store, a fashion store and a menswear store. I learned that each store was different. I had a different style for each one. I knew what clothes to sell in each store. I knew how to display the clothes. The stores were successful. A restaurant is the same. You made a big mistake. You tried to make a lunchtime restaurant for businessmen. But this restaurant is all wrong. The style is wrong and the menu is wrong. I understand you wanted to get new customers and younger people. But restaurants are like fashion. You have to know what to sell, and how to display it.

"You have to choose. If you want the lunchtime businessmen, you will need a normal lunchtime restaurant menu. You will have to change the décor. But I don't think you will be successful. I heard Mr Kimura has found a place near here to open a restaurant. He will be much more successful than you."

"Oh no!" cried Akiko. "We will have to close this restaurant."

"Maybe not," said Mrs Wada. "You are young married women. You designed this restaurant for young women. You didn't design the restaurant for businessmen. You thought about yourselves, not the customers."

"Wada san, I understand you," said Amy. "It is good advice. But we have a problem. This restaurant is in the business area of town. We have no car park. Only office workers who work in buildings near here will come."

"There are many young people who work in offices near here," answered Mrs Wada.

"They will come if they think it is fashionable. Not every day, but sometimes. Also, as you know, I own this building. There are six parking spaces next door. I own those parking spaces. I will let you use them for six months. After that, you must pay 4,000 yen a month for each one."

"You are so kind!" cried Amy. "Please don't think I am rude, but why are you helping us?"

"After I married my husband, I got a bad shock. He was lazy. He didn't like to work and he was not very smart. Soon I had three small children, and there was no money. I had to do something for my children. I opened a clothes shop. We lived behind the shop. I could work in the shop and watch my children too. It was very hard. I made many mistakes. I often cried and could not sleep at night. When I came here with my friends, I saw that you were very worried. I knew that the restaurant was not a success. I remembered what it was like for me. I thought I would help you."

"You're very kind," said Akiko. "But we have made a bad start. I know you are right but I don't know how to change things."

"First, you must change the menu. Do not have curry rice and noodles. Have modern interesting food. Have low calorie salads and healthy raw food. I also think you should have more delicious cakes on the menu. One of my friends is always on a diet. She will eat a lettuce leaf for lunch, but then she will have chocolate cake with coffee.

"Then you must have a big event. Something that will get your restaurant in the local newspaper."

"What kind of event?" asked Amy. "What do you suggest?"

Mrs Wada smiled. "You must think about that yourselves. If I help you any more it will not be your business." She stood up. "I will tell my son to arrange the parking spaces. Good luck."

9. AKIKO HAS AN IDEA

Akiko was standing in her kitchen. It was very early on Saturday morning. Her restaurant didn't open on Saturdays or Sundays.

If I don't do something soon, it will not be open any day, thought Akiko.

Akiko thought Mrs Wada was right. The restaurant was for young married women. But the restaurant was in the office area of town. How could she and Amy get young people to come to the restaurant? Mrs Wada told them to have a big event. A very big event. Something to get a story in the newspapers. It was a good idea. But what event? If Akiko or Amy did not have a clever idea soon, the restaurant would have to close down. It was costing too much money and they had no customers.

Akiko heard a noise near the door of her apartment. It was the man delivering the newspaper.

She went to the door and collected the newspaper. She took the newspaper and put it on the counter in the kitchen. She poured herself a cup of coffee and started to read the paper.

On the entertainment page, there was an article about the movie *Two Worlds – One Love.* It was about a young Japanese doctor who falls in love with an American student. The movie had been filmed in both Japan and America.

Last year, Akiko and Amy had gone to the premiere of this movie. It had been a very exciting weekend. They had met the star of the movie. They had stayed in the Ritz-Carlton hotel and gone to the premiere party. All this had happened because Amy's mother was planning to marry Homer, the movie producer.

It seemed a long time ago.

I must be positive, thought Akiko. *Amazing things happen all the time. I never believed I would go to a movie premiere and meet a famous actor, but I did. I must believe in good luck.*

Akiko read the article. The movie was very popular. It was a big success.

---All over Japan, young people are imagining that they are the student. Kenta Nakamura, who plays the part of the doctor in the film, has become an idol...---

He is very handsome, thought Akiko. *Could I put a sign in the window of the restaurant that says 'Come and talk to us! We met Kenta Nakamura!'*

Then Akiko had an idea. *No! Not a notice! A sign that says 'Meet Kenta Nakamura'!*

Akiko was in her pyjamas. She didn't stop to change. She took the newspaper and ran out of her apartment. She ran to Amy's apartment and rang the bell.

No one answered. "Hurry! Hurry! Answer the door!" she shouted. Akiko was so excited she couldn't wait.

Finally Dick came to the door. He was in his pyjamas too.

"Akiko! Hi! What's wrong?"

Akiko ran into the apartment. "Amy! Amy! Wake up! I have a wonderful idea!"

Dick laughed. "I'll make coffee," he said.

Amy came out of the bedroom. Akiko hugged her. "Amy! Listen! You have to call Homer!"

"What? Akiko, calm down."

Amy took Akiko into the living room. They sat on the sofa.

"Listen! I have had a wonderful idea!"

Akiko explained. "Remember the movie we went to in Osaka? Look here in the newspaper. The movie is a great success. The star, Kenta Nakamura, has become very famous. Young women like him very much. You can ask Homer to tell Kenta Nakamura to come here. To our restaurant! We will be in all the newspapers and our restaurant will be famous!"

Amy thought about it. "But Akiko, Homer might say 'no'. Or Kenta Nakamura might say 'no'."

"We have to ask," said Akiko. "Please Amy, will you call Homer and ask him?"

Amy was smiling. "I don't know if he will say 'yes' or 'no'. But if he says 'yes', it will be wonderful! It's the middle of the afternoon on

Friday in California. It's a good time to call. I'll do it now."

Amy called Homer. She talked for a long time. When she finished she jumped up and down. Then she hugged Akiko. Dick came in with a tray of coffee. She hugged Dick too.

"Stop! Stop! I'll drop the coffee!" said Dick.

"Akiko is a genius!" shouted Amy. "Homer thinks it is a good idea. He loves publicity. He says our city is small, but Kenta's visit will be on television. So everyone in this part of Japan will see it. He says that in the movie, the young doctor comes from a small city. He thinks it is perfect. He will call Kenta Nakamura today. He will tell him to do it. Homer's company will arrange everything."

It was almost 10:30am before Akiko went back to her apartment. Seiji was still sleeping.

I will cook something very special for lunch, thought Akiko. *Today is a very special day.*

10. A GRAND RE-OPENING

The next week, Seiji, Dick, Akiko and Amy ate dinner together in Amy and Dick's apartment. Dick had made his special curry.

"I have news," said Amy. "Kenta Nakamura's agent called me. Kenta is very happy to come. Kenta comes from a small city, so he will enjoy visiting this city. The agent said that Kenta remembered us from the party!"

"Oh, Amy," laughed Dick. "Big stars have to say things like that."

"Yes, maybe. But the agent said that Kenta remembered the cute Japanese woman in the red dress. Akiko wore a red dress to the party!"

"Oh, no!" said Seiji. "I will have to come to the restaurant when Kenta Nakamura is there. I will take a day's vacation. I don't want him to steal my wife."

"You don't have to worry," Akiko smiled at Seiji. "I am very happy with my wonderful husband. He is handsome, but you are more handsome than him."

Seiji was very pleased.

It took about three weeks to arrange everything. There were many articles in the newspaper about Kenta Nakamura's visit to the city. The city where Akiko and Amy live is small. It is very unusual to have important visitors, so everyone in the city was talking about it.

But Akiko and Amy had some trouble. So many important people in the city wanted to come to their restaurant on the day of the visit. Even the Mayor wanted to come.

"It will be very good for his image to have a photograph with

Kenta Nakamura," said Dick.

Akiko and Amy didn't know what to do. All the powerful people wanted to come but Akiko and Amy wanted young people there too.

Then the newspaper sent a man to see them.

"We would like to have a competition," he said. "It is for young people. There will be six prize-winners. The prize will be to have lunch in this restaurant, the day Kenta Nakamura comes. We will call the competition 'Meet the star! Lunch with Kenta Nakamura!' Of course we will pay for the lunches."

Akiko and Amy cooked and cooked and cooked. Amy created a new dessert – it was an ice cream cake in two flavours. She called the dessert *Two worlds –One love.*

Amy planned to make vases of flowers for the tables. But she didn't have to. A florist came to see them.

"We will do all the flowers for the restaurant for free. We want you to put our business cards on the tables. The business cards say, 'Flowers by Rose. Flowers for every occasion'. Our telephone number is on the card too," said the florist.

Then the big day came. There were television cameras and radio reporters. There were hundreds of people on the street. The local brass band came. When the limousine arrived at the restaurant and Kenta Nakamura got out, the band played the theme song from the movie *Two Worlds – One Love.*

Kenta Nakamura was wonderful. He talked to everyone outside the restaurant. He smiled for the cameras. He talked to the television people.

He said, "I know Akiko and Amy. I met them in Osaka. I am looking forward to eating lunch. I am sure it will be delicious."

The restaurant was full. In the middle was a big table. Kenta Nakamura ate lunch with the Mayor at that table. Also at the big table was Mrs Wada. She was very pleased. Mrs Wada and her friends often went to the movies. All the other tables in the restaurant were full too.

Lunch was a great success. Kenta Nakamura ate a lot. He said that everything tasted very good. He said the food was fresh and healthy. The Mayor ate a lot too. Mrs Wada did not eat very much, but she looked very happy.

Everyone said good things about the food.

In the kitchen, Seiji and Dick were working hard. They had a special job.

"The camera men, sound men, drivers and assistants have a hard time," said Seiji. "I think we should feed them as well."

So Akiko and Amy prepared big trays of food and drink. Dick and Seiji carried the trays out the back door of the restaurant and took them to all the workers outside. Then they carried out trays of cakes. Every cake was wrapped in paper. The paper said: ---*Thank you for coming today. Come and see us again at Tuscany*---

Dick and Seiji gave the cakes to all the fans waiting on the street.

Finally, the event finished. Akiko, Amy, Seiji and Dick were very tired. They closed the door of the restaurant and sat down.

"I have news!" said Akiko.

"No. No. No news!" said Amy. "I am too tired. And the restaurant has reservations every day for the next month. We have to cook tomorrow."

"But listen!" said Akiko. "Mrs Wada spoke to me before she left. She said we had been very clever. She said we did well. She said if we want to open another restaurant she will be our partner."

Dick, Amy and Seiji turned and looked at Akiko.

Then they all shouted together, "No way!"

Then Amy said, "Well, not yet!"

THANK YOU

Thank you for reading Akiko and Amy Part 3. (Word count: 10,374)
We hope you enjoyed it.

If you would like to read more graded readers, please visit our
website http://www.italkyoutalk.com

Other Level 3 graded readers include
A Dangerous Weekend
A Holiday to Remember
Akiko and Amy Part 1
Akiko and Amy Part 2
Be My Valentine
Different Seas
Enjoy Your Business Trip
Enjoy Your Homestay
I Need a Friend
Old Jack's Ghost Stories from England (1)
Old Jack's Ghost Stories from England (2)
Old Jack's Ghost Stories from Ireland
Old Jack's Ghost Stories from Japan
Old Jack's Ghost Stories from Scotland
Old Jack's Ghost Stories from Wales
Party Time!
Stories for Christmas
The Curse

Together Again
Who is Holly?

ABOUT THE AUTHOR

I Talk You Talk Press is a Japan-based publisher of language textbooks, graded readers and language learning/teaching resources.

Our team is made up of highly experienced language teachers and translators, who have all studied at least one additional language to an advanced level.

This experience enables us to design our materials from the perspective of both the teacher and the learner. We consult with both teachers and language learners when designing our textbooks and graded readers, and test our materials extensively in the classroom before publication.

We are a fast-growing press, and currently publish graded readers for learners of English. We publish new graded readers monthly.

www.ingramcontent.com/pod-product-compliance
Lightning Source LLC
Chambersburg PA
CBHW022348040426
42449CB00006B/779